A Quick and Bloody Affair:
The Skirmish at Torrence's Tavern

O.C. Stonestreet IV

Dedication

This book is dedicated to the memory of Mrs. Margaret Shoe. Her passion for Colonial History lives on in the lives of an entire generation of former students. On behalf of myself, and the entire history department at Mooresville Senior High School, thank you for all of your many years of service and friendship.

Acknowledgments

I want to thank several individuals, and groups, for their assistance in this venture. Thank you to the lovely ladies in the Davidson College Archive for their continued assistance over the many years. Rev. Dr. Gus Succop for his friendship and kind support. Dan Thorp, Associate Professor of History at Virginia Tech for his fantastic help on tavern history and culture. Thank you to Kathy O'Neil and Deb Speaks of the Mary Slocumb Chapter of the DAR for their endless friendship, and willingness to assist in research and photography. To Anne Hobbs and Mary Morrow for reminding me that a historian always investigates further. Dr. Hugh Dussek at Central Piedmont Community College for his years of support. A special thank you to Mrs. April Davala for her time and watchful literary eye. Damien Akleman at MHS for tech support. Thank you to all of the DAR, SAR, and SR members… for you keep history alive for other generations. Thank you to Mr. Will Graves for his fantastic work. Lastly, a special thank you to all my family, colleagues, and friends.

Contents

Seven Miles North of Cowan's Ford

" The colonel rode up and looked all of us in the eye confident as he passed by on his on his mottled gray horse. We could see in the distance, people fleeing our advance along the road towards Salisbury. A few mounted rebel militia rode towards us; at which our skirmishers fired upon driving them back to their lines. As we formed from column to an adjusted line of five horsemen a breast to accommodate the road, these men opposite us some 150 yards away were forming a line behind overturned wagons along a fence near what looked like a small settlement.

It began to rain when Colonel Tarleton's mount stopped pacing. As he wheeled about to face the lead men just in front of us, all of us heard him say in a loud and sharp voice…

' We have pushed the rebels back from the ford to Tarrant's Crossroads which lies ahead of you. We have killed their general, now let's stab their hearts and their hopes! For King and Country'… "REMEMBER THE COWPENS! "

At that, the colonel jolted his mount and drew his sword, which made a distinct sound. He always seemed to have a swagger that excited us all, and we braced ourselves as the charge was ordered. As the advance quickened, it sounded like thunder as we went from a trot to a gallop in this wet reddish mud. As the road opened wider near the community, our second line instinctively fanned out. We were now 10 to 15 men abreast. We had scarcely reached our speed when the rebel line let loose a volley that seemed like a sheet of fire. Practically, all of our forward line buckled, horses were screaming as they were hit. Our other lines had to jump over or try to pivot around these fallen lads. We could not stop. At that, a second volley was loosed into our line. Colonel Tarleton, not wanting to break off and lose the initiative, ordered us to wheel left like a snake and then we came at the rebel line from the oblique towards their center. With increased anger, we pierced their line within moments.

The rebels immediately started to flee. We sabred many in their backs when they took to their heels. The colonel then ordered B company to 'chase and pursue' as far as advisable. Within moments it was over. Our Royal Provincial Legion had proved its bravery, yet at a high cost. Some twenty horses, and seven men were killed, and another seven or so men injured in the charge. We quickly realized the Patriot militia was prepared for our attack and were not 'routed from the ford' as the colonel had thought. These rebels were determined to put up a fight. Had the light rains not dampened the rebel's powder, and our speed not been in our favor, the fight would have been a great contest.

Our wounded were being treated, and a few rebel prisoners being questioned, when I saw some troopers running out of the tavern with plunder. Other men with torches approached the widow's tavern to set the place to fire. Tarleton was giving orders to 'keep moving' as his outline was clear against the smoldering blaze engulfing the buildings and wagons behind him.

- Tarrant's Cross Roads, Afternoon 1st Feb. 1781.

Lifting the Fog of History

As a boy growing up in a rural part of Iredell County, I had heard about of the Battle of Cowan's Ford and the fight at Torrence's Tavern. My father had the habit of taking me on adventures during the weekends at a time when I was not very interested in local history. Being the child of a history teacher sort of made me the tag along or "reluctant assistant" in local history research. Looking back, I am not sure what I was really interested in at nine years old other than Legos, but something must have stuck. As time went on, I found myself changing from an art major to a history major while at Wingate College (now Wingate University) in the 1980s. Little did I realize, while working on a masters some fifteen years later, these stories from my youth would lead to several books on local history. My father had won out after all.

I remember a program presented by the 'late and great' Paul Harvey called "*The Rest of the Story.*" This radio show aired during the week on the ABC Radio Network. The program told little known facts of great people and events. Radio commentator Paul Harvey wove a fantastic narrative of uncommon knowledge and trivia for those who were interested in knowing more about a famous subject. Likewise, I see this work in the same light. My other works on the Battle of Colson's Mill and the Battle of Cowan's Ford tell the core narrative of the fighting that stretched between the Pee Dee and the Catawba River areas during the American Revolutionary War. This work, however, is a bit different. Certainly for a person interested in the Southern Campaign of the American Revolutionary War, it is yet another historic jewel to recount. However, this work is not just a story about past events, it is one of current events as well, and the efforts to save local history for future memory.

It was not long after the publication of my book on the Battle of Colson's Mill that I had questions posed to me about working on another dealing with the skirmish at Torrence's Tavern. Many friends and members of the local DAR Chapter had asked, and my response was simply, "There was not enough information to do it." Little did I realize these fantastic ladies were placing seeds in my mind that it could be done, and there was more out there than I had originally thought. One of my oldest and best friends Kathy O'Neil said prophetically, "You know you are going to do it." At the last meeting of the Mary Slocumb Chapter of the DAR in June, 2014 I realized Kathy was right. Anne Hobbs and Mary Morrow, two very dedicated and patriotic ladies of the local DAR chapter, sat right beside me. A discussion ensued and both ladies started brainstorming about what they knew of the tavern. The very next day, Mrs. Morrow placed several pages from a genealogical article in my mailbox at the high school. Like my father, they had won out and I realized that I had not really looked into it.

I had held in my mind what many people in Mooresville and Iredell region had known about the battle since they were young, "General Davidson lost his life at Cowan's Ford, and a handful of men fled to Torrence's Tavern and were surprised by the British troops while patching up their wounds. Then, the militia melted away… end of story." "I am a poor historian," as I thought to myself. Maybe there is more material on the skirmish out there, and thus more to the story after all.

Other than published works, the question would be where to look? I had the fortunate occurrence to run across a fantastic set of databases, which had transcribed pension records from the Revolutionary War. These veteran pension applications from the 1830s to the 1850s were the key. As I said in my other works, these firsthand accounts are a true goldmine for researchers interested in the American Revolution. Thankfully, there are those out there who have the drive and time to transcribe extremely difficult 19th century records and establish databases to help lowly historians such as myself. People like Nancy Poquette and Will Graves, two historians and pension transcribers have dedicated hundreds, if not thousands, of hours to preserving American History.

Sure enough, I typed in "Torrence's Tavern" to scan their records and I had hits. Not only did I find it as Torrence's Tavern, but I realized this landmark went by many other names during the Colonial Era: Tarrant's Tavern, Tarrant's Lane, Tarrant's

Crossroads, Tarrant's Hall and the Widow Torrence's Tavern or Lane. One would think this would be a nightmare for a researcher, yet it is a gift. By having various names, this broadened the scope of who might have recorded a memory while applying for a pension. Little did I know it would also lead to solving a great mystery as well!

It took several months just to print and plow through the many records. What became apparent was this fight at Torrence's (or Tarrant's) was not what we 'locals' had thought it was for over two centuries. Slowly but surely, fantastic nuggets of information from first and second hand accounts painted a different picture of the importance of the fight, and what actually occurred. The fog of history began to lift, and the search for historic truth began.

The Retreat from Cowan's Ford

Captain Erwin's men were moving forward towards the bank of the river where the night before a small party of men had been placed as skirmishers. Now, shots and shouts rang out along the bank. The militia was still groggy when they made their way in feverous haste to the sounds in the waning darkness. About the time militiaman John Baldwin was approaching the ridge, he could see young men coming towards him through the pine trees in panic. Just then General Davidson and Colonel Polk, with a handful of men, bolted past Baldwin. He could hear the general urging his men to make a stand, and trying to get a gage of the overall situation.

A young boy ran past Davidson screaming, 'the Brits are on the bank!' Baldwin and some of his militia had just caught up with Davidson when he saw the shapes of men lowering their weapons. It was as if the enemy had materialized out of the river itself. More of them came out of the water towards the bank with their weapons held high. Horses could be heard struggling against the fast current of the Catawba River.

Baldwin was priming the pan of his musket when he heard Davidson's commanding shouts from twenty yards away for the men to fall back. Suddenly, a volley was fired from the darkness. In an instant, it seemed to Baldwin that the entire bank of the Catawba was a flame. Then he saw Davidson buckle in pain and fall from his horse, landing twisted on the ground beside Colonel Polk. Baldwin heard what he thought was German, and could see outlines of men rushing up the ridge. Shaking, he fired at a moving shape and then as fast as he could, he headed towards the tavern, praying more militia were willing to make a stand with the tavern defenders.[1]

John Baldwin was one of several militiamen who recounted Davidson's final moments in their pension application. General Davidson's martyrdom for the Patriot cause has been almost mythologized in North Carolina history now for over two centuries. Through the 19th Century, his stand on the Catawba

---

[1] John Baldwin, Pension Application Transcribed by Will Graves-
http://revwarapps.org/s31402.pdf (Retrieved: 07/21/2014) S6565 fn10NC

found its way into patriotic speeches, textbooks, and at various civic commemorations. Most accounts agree to Davidson's final moments with great similarity. Yet, what happened to Davidson's men at Torrent's Tavern after his death has been seen as a simple footnote to the larger story. When I started researching the events surrounding Torrence's Tavern, I realized there existed one or two accounts that had become "historic gospel" to myself and many Carolinians. Those works being the histories presented by Gen. Joseph Graham and historian John H. Wheeler.

Even with the popularity of these historic works, there were some who criticized their interpretation of specific events. As mentioned in my other book, *The Battle of Cowan's Ford*, a young militiaman named Robert Henry took issue with Wheeler's take on Davidson's stand because Henry had been there during the action as a 16 year old volunteer. A bestseller in the mid 19th Century, John Wheeler's: *Historical sketches of North Carolina: from 1584 to 1851, compiled from original records, official documents and traditional statements; with biographical sketches* is a massive work. Yet, Henry's own account of the action along the Catawba is replete with critiques against Wheeler on several specific points. Henry even challenges the importance of then 'Captain' (later General) Joseph Graham had in the ensuing action, as recorded by Wheeler. [2]

General Graham's own accounts and communications of the war were later collected, sorted and printed in: *General Joseph Graham and his Papers on North Carolina Revolutionary History* in 1904 by a descendant. These documents gave many people an insight into the American Revolutionary War from the view of one man who had fought gallantly in it. It seems between Graham's account of the war, in tandem with Wheeler's work, became what many Carolinians regarded as historic gospel when dealing with Cowan's Ford and the skirmish at Torrence's Tavern.

As I delved deeper into the various pension narratives, it became clear that unlike General Davidson's final moments, the actions surrounding the retreat and the stand at the tavern

---

[2] O.C. Stonestreet IV, The Battle of Cowan's Ford: General Davidson's Stand on the Catawba River and its Place in North Carolina History, (Createspace, Charleston 2012) p. 16.

varied greatly. This is not to say either Wheeler or Graham were intentionally trying to deceive the public, but rather they were mostly acting on 'hearsay' to events at which they were not a direct witnesses. Even in Graham's case during the war, his recounting would have been from a singular point of view. [3]

The pension records revealed that Torrence's Tavern had been a gathering spot for men and supplies in the weeks prior to the Battle at Cowan's Ford. Not only Torrence's, but many other taverns and camps along the main thoroughfares of the south had become makeshift storage areas and landmarks for regional Patriot militias. A true gem of history I ran across was a general "Call to Arms" in the papers of Colonel Samuel Hammond. It mentions Torrence's in passing, and the need for assistance. It gives an insight into the patriotic spirit, and the need for civic support during the war:

---

[3] Dare I say it? John H. Wheeler was a politician.

"A Call to Arms: Beef, Bread & Potatoes
Higgins' Plantation 23rd, Sept. 1780

   The undersigned has just returned from Hillsborough to this
neighborhood. While there he obtained an order on the
Companies and Quartermaster upon this frontier for supplies of
provisions and forage for such of the patriotic Citizens of South
Carolina and Georgia as might be embodied for actual services
and being informed that there is a number of you, resisting with
patriotic friends in the Two adjoining Counties no doubt
anxiously looking for an opportunity to embody for the
performance of duty, but without the power or means of
supporting yourselves or your horses from your own resources I
have thought your wishes would be forwarded by the
Establishing of a Camp at a rallying rendezvous at a convenient
place for your assemblage, and to be ready when occasion might
offer to give our aid for recovery of Our Country.

I have with this view formed a camp at Higgin's Plantation a few
miles from Capt. Brannon's Tavern, near the road leading
westerly to Torrence's Crossroads, where we will be supplied
with the needful. I am justified in the expectation of the arrival of
a powerful support shortly and that we may return home with a
strong army. Let us be prepared to do our part, our little force
will be important if combined possessing as we do a better
knowledge of the County and its resources. Now is the time to
show ourselves and I invite you, both Officers & Soldiers to obey
the call: I here assure you that I shall cheerfully surrender the
Command, and Cooperate fully to and with any Officer of Senior
Rank of wither State that may think proper to join; Should an
opportunity offer immediately for my advancing toward the
enemy with a prospect of doing good and officer will be left at
this Camp authorized to obtain Rations? For such as may Join

there after my departing. I have some other good news. Come and hear it.

> S. Hammond (Major)
> Comdg. Refugees Lower Regt." [4]

One can see that Hammond was trying to drum up support of both men and supplies. His words evidently did not fall on deaf ears. John Baldwin mentions that Torrence's Tavern itself had been a depository for supplies utilized by various militias.[5] As mentioned in historian Dan Thorp's article on *Taverns and Tavern Culture on the Southern Colonial Frontier: Rowan County, North Carolina*, taverns were extremely important to communities, and served a variety of purposes during peacetime. One can only imagine how important they would become in a time of conflict.[6]

Men were retreating towards Torrence's Tavern from both Cowan's and Beatties Ford once the British forces had breached

---

[4] Samuel Hammond, Pension Application Transcribed by Will Graves- http://revwarapps.org/s31402.pdf (Retrieved: 07/19/2014) S21087 f84SC (p. 81)

[5] John Baldwin, Pension application transcribed by Will Graves - http://revwarapps.org/s31402.pdf (Retrieved:07/21, 2014) S6565 fn10NC (p.1).

[6] Daniel B. Thorp, Taverns and Tavern Culture on the Southern Colonial Frontier: Rowan County, North Carolina, 1753-1776. *The Journal of Southern History,* Vol. 62. No. 4(Nov., 1996), PP. 661-688. http://www.jstor.org/stable/2211137. Retrieved: 19/12/2013.

the other side of the river. Lord Cornwallis had a small detachment sent to bombard Beatties Ford with a British 'three pounder' as a diversionary *feint* from across the river. Now in the morning light, the Patriot detachment stationed there soon realized they were not the primary objective. To make matters difficult for the men at Beatties, once the lead elements of Lord Cornwallis force was across the Catawba, his Lordship had dispatched the 23th Foot towards the main road just east of the ford. This, added to the fact that more civilians were now starting to flee along the main road, hampered the Patriot's return back to the tavern rally-point.[7] Cornwallis relays an account of the action to Lord Germain:

"I detached Lieut. Colonel Tarleton with the Cavalry and 23rd Regiment to pursue the routed Militia. A few were soon killed or taken and Lieut. Colonel Tarleton having learned that 3 or 400 of the neighboring Militia were to assemble that day at Tarrant's

---

[7] Lieutenant-General Tarleton CN, *A History of the Campaigns of 1780 and 1781, in the Southern Provinces of North America*, London, 1787, (Reprint- Public Domain, 2014)., p.225. Also note that Davidson had knowledge of the 23rd Foot Reg. via intelligence received prior to Cowan's Ford. (British Archives and Davidson College Special Collections)

house, about ten miles from the ford. Leaving his Infantry he went on with the Cavalry and finding the Militia as expected, he with excellent conduct and great spirit, attacked them instantly and totally routed them, with little loss on his side; and on theirs between forty and fifty killed, wounded or prisoners." [8]

-Gen. Cornwallis to Lord Germain
  March 17th, 1781

Once men from the various forward areas started to reach the tavern, the picture Graham and Wheeler depict for us becomes a bit more complex when one starts looking into other firsthand accounts. If one looks at Graham's account, the long-held version of events comes to mind. In less than three pages he mentions how 'Widow Torrence' became a widow, how some retreating men were drinking quantities of rum after Cowan's, and how these men were then surprised by Col. Tarleton's sudden appearance. Graham does, however, take time to mention one 'Captain Nathaniel Martin' was unfortunate enough to have his

---

[8] Cornwallis to Germain, March 17th, 1781, *The Cornwallis Papers,* Letter from Charles Cornwallis, Marquis Cornwallis to George Sackville Germain, Viscount Sackville Volume 17, http://docsouth.unc.edu/csr/index.html/document/csr17-0307 (Retrieved 08/04/2014), pp. 998-999.

horse shot out from under him, and was taken captive. He also gives statistics like ten Patriots were killed in the ensuing fight. Then his narrative moves on to other topics. [9]

Yet the pension applications of the 1830s, along with other accounts (Cornwallis and Tarleton), frame a very different story. It is not one of scared men trying to calm their nerves with large quantities of alcohol and then suddenly surprised by Tarleton's Green Dragoons at all. I am sure men who were in transition from the forward areas toward the tavern would have been surprised, given the road conditions and the speed at which the British cavalry force had reached the area. However, for the men stationed at the tavern as a secondary defense line, it was no surprise at all. They were waiting, and certainly on guard, once the first men returned from the Catawba and alerted them the British had reached the near bank. Many of the pension accounts list troops having visited or stationed at the tavern in the weeks

---

[9] William A. Graham, *General Joseph Graham and his Papers on North Carolina Revolutionary History; with Appendix: An Epitome of North Carolina's Military Services in the Revolutionary War and of the Laws Enacted for Raising Troops,* Miami: Hard Press Publishing, (Print on Demand 2013), 1904 ed. Pp. 298-300. Note: Widow Torrence lost her husband at the Battle of Ramsour's Mill the month before.-Possibly Adam Torrence Sr.

leading up to the stand on the Catawba River. Interestingly enough, even Col. Tarleton's own account notes the tavern defenders were well prepared for an assault:

" Although the report of the distance and the numbers contrary to his wishes, he (Tarleton) reflected, that the time was advantageous to make (an) impression upon the militia; that the weather, on account of a violent rain, was favorable for the project; and that a retreat was always practicable with a superior body of cavalry. Actuated by these considerations, he determined by rapid march, to approach the enemy; The militia were vigilant, and were prepared for an attack." [10]

- Tarleton's Memoirs

---

[10] Tarleton, pp. 225-226.

This 'Dragoon Helmet' is in the collection at the North Carolina Museum of History. This is probably from the War of 1812, yet its style is somewhat based on a design attributed to Tarleton. The long Napoleonic braided plumes were stylish. Yet, they were to serve as a simple protection for the trooper's neck if assaulted by a sabre... at least in theory. (Photo: Author's Collection)

A Quick and Bloody Affair

As Col. Tarleton's troops moved down the road to within sight of Torrence's Tavern, he weighed his options. The infantry who had been assigned to support him had fallen behind due to the roads becoming muddy in the recent rains. Like all good cavalry commanders, Tarleton understood he had two main tasks. Besides being the "eyes of the army," his other main task was to break up enemy forces from regrouping. However he did debated on fully committing to the assault, having seen the defenses at the tavern himself. Overturned wagons, and a fence line spanned the western side of the tavern's property. The Patriot militia was already in place behind the fence, and more men scrambled out of the tavern and adjacent buildings towards the wall.

Tarleton realized he still held the initiative but not for long. The longer he waited for reinforcements, so too were the Patriot militia gaining support and bracing themselves for an advance. The militia sent a few riders out towards Tarleton's troops, probably as a simple reconnaissance. Yet, they were soon driven back to the tavern lines by a few shots from the legion's skirmishers.

Col. Tarleton also saw a chance to regain some of the prestige that his legion had lost in recent engagements. Turning to his men, he made an impromptu and impassioned speech ending with… *"Remember the Cowpens!"*[11] At that, the charge was ordered: " Tarleton resolved to hazard one charge, and, if unsuccessful, order a retreat."[12] The legionnaires drew their swords and started to charge in 'line abreast' that fanned out as they increasingly rushed towards the tavern's defenders. [13]

The account of Tarleton's ferocious attack has never been in question, but there still exists many questions about the militia defenders at this critical point. As mentioned, Gen. Graham gives the view of surprise and unpreparedness. Though Tarleton's own account, along with Patriot narratives, presents an entirely

---

10. Tarleton, p.226.

[12] Ibid, p.226.

[13] Many place pistols or a type of carbine musket in the hands of Tarleton's men. Yet the sabre was designed for the swift attack. It was the cavalryman's main weapon. Pistols and muskets only offered one shot and would have been wasted in any such swift attack. (I am also speaking as a former fencing instructor rated in the sabre).

different scene. When reviewing the many pension records, one comes to the conclusion it was an intense and violent fight that lasted around twenty minutes or less; and a number of prisoners besides Capt. Martin were taken. [14]

Veteran Elijah Dollar recalled part of Gen. Davidson's force were stationed at Torrence's Tavern as a secondary defensive line against the British:

" The American forces were on this side of the River & the British on the other, sometime after (the) applicant was marched thither, & before the British crossed to the North side & had on occasion with a portion of the American forces under General Davidson, the declarant was marched to Torrence's Tavern. At the time of that engagement, this declarant & about 400 of the Americans were stationed at Torrence's Tavern, as well as he remembers the same, some 7 or 8 miles from the scene of action." Dollar goes on to state that, " Shortly after the battle, the British Dragoons charged the Americans at Torrence's Tavern several times—and at the time of the second charge, the

---

[14] This includes the pursuit of skirmishers sent out once the tavern defenders broke into retreating groups.

declarant was taken prisoner by the war. He was carried by them as a prisoner first to Salisbury & there lodged in Jail...." [15]

Notice Dollar's account not only stresses a fairly large amount of militia stationed at the tavern, but also the difficulty the assaulting force had in the initial attack. Graham's account mentioning only one prisoner being taken is certainly incorrect due to Dollar being taken as a prisoner of war as well during the battle. Dollar gives a detailed account of where he was taken and held as the British moved east before making his daring escape a few weeks later. [16]

It is true that Capt. Martin was captured in the opening stages of Tarleton's assault. It is well documented Martin had his horse shot out form under him, and he was possibly penned beneath his fallen mount. Veteran Jonas Clark recalled, " He (Clark) had volunteered with Capt. Martin and others who joined our company and continued to harass the British on their march and at Mrs. Torrens' (Torrence's) at the cross roads we had a smart

---

[15] Elijiah Dollar, Pension Application Transcribed by Will Graves-
http://revwarapps.org/s31402.pdf (Retrieved: 07/21/2014) W17729 fn34NC If at all possible, cavalry would veer versus breaking completely off an advance, or possibly the British 23rd Foot had come up to support them as they regrouped.
[16] Ibid, p. 2 of the pension application.

skirmish were our Captain Martin had his horse killed and himself taken prisoner and Robert Walker, the lieutenant, took command of his company."[17]

Graham may have heard from others only a few details of the initial attack, and it is understandable many defenders fled their lines were once the defenses were breached. Their orders were only to act as a delaying action, and not one of 'hold every inch of ground until the last.' There is very good evidence the British infantry assigned to Tarleton (23rd Foot) had possibly caught up with Tarleton's cavalry during the last stages of the engagement with a fast-paced march. Pensioner Benjamin Shaw mentions both cavalry and Infantry in the assault. [18] Veteran James Neil goes on to claimed some 300 Patriots were at the tavern to face any British forces that appeared after their crossing. One thing does become clear with a review of the firsthand accounts. There were more than just a few stranglers at the tavern when Tarleton's troops arrived.

[17] Jonas Clark, Pension Application Transcribed by Will Graves- http://revwarapps.org/s31402.pdf (Retrieved: 07/21/2014) W1386 fn87SC

[18] Benjamin Shaw , Pension Application Transcribed by Will Graves- http://revwarapps.org/s31402.pdf (Retrieved: 07/21/2014) S3885 fn27NC   (See also Sargent Lamb's account with the 23rd Foot..)

As far as the consumption of alcohol as mentioned in Graham's narrative, it was common practice in the British Army to distribute a bit of gin or "on the job gin" to calm the nerves of soldiers prior to a major battle. [19] Certainly, many of the militia that fought at the fords may have had a serving of what the tavern had on hand, but the "pails and buckets full" certainly portray their actions in a different light than a simple case of calming their nerves, or steadying them for an impeding fight. Veteran Elias Lovelace mentions only "... at which place (Torrence's Taven) they got refreshments and then proceeded on towards Guilford...."[20] I believe the tale of the defenders pilfering drinks is greatly exaggerated when one looks at the timing and their actions in the skirmish. One must remember that for much of the militia, this was their first taste of battle. Certainly, this was a stressful event that may have caused some to have a drink. Naturally, there were some militiamen who had served multiple enlistments in other campaigns. I am sure these

[19] Our current phrase "feeling groggy " comes from a watered mix of alcohol and water served to British sailors. The "grog", if consumed in large quantitates, could cause a stupor.
[20] Elias Lovelace, Pension Application Transcribed by Will Graves- http://revwarapps.org/s31402.pdf (Retrieved: 08/21/2014).

veterans came forward to act as leaders, and to steady the others. This brings up another interesting question with no clear answer. Considering the death of General Davidson, who was in command at Torrence's Tavern?

For years, it was assumed that Capt. Martin was in command. From Graham's account, one imagines the image of a plucky young man on a horse giving orders until a volley unhorsed him. [21] However, there were many at the tavern that had equal or greater rank than Capt. Martin. Just looking at a few of the pension records, many names of officers are placed either in command, or at the scene during the action. The following officers have been listed in one or more accounts as being involved in the affair: Captain Nathaniel (also known as Salathiel) Martin, Captain Erwin, Captain Armstrong, Captain Thomas Cowan, Colonel Thomas Farmer, and Colonel (recently promoted to general) Andrew Pickens. The following are

---

[21] Several pension records claim that Nathaniel (Salathiel) was well over six feet tall. He would have been an imposing figure in the 18th Century when the average height of a man was around 5 foot 6 inches.

excerpts from several pension accounts shedding some light on who might have been in command?

John Baldwin   28th August, 1832

"(John Baldwin) – and soon entered the service as a Substitute for his uncle John Badlwin in the North Carolina Militia under the same Captain Erwin and Joined a body of Militia for the purpose of preventing Cornwallis from crossing the Catawba River…. This declarant with a party of men retreated to one Mr. Torrence's where were deposited some public Stores & here they were soon attacked & dispersed by a parcel of British Dragoons." [22]

Polly Brandon (Widow) of Benjamin Brandon 20th March, 1844

" He (Benjamin Brandon) the proceeded under General Davidson & was present & took part in the Battle of Cowan's Ford, in which action General Davidson fell. This was on the Catawba

---

[22] John Baldwin, Pension Application Transcribed by Will Graves- http://revwarapps.org/s31402.pdf (Retrieved: 07/21/2014) S6565 fn10NC

River & under the command of Captain Abel Armstrong (under Col. Locke). He was also at the defeat of the American troops at Torrence's Cross Roads, under the last named Captain."

Benjamin Carroll   30th May, 1833

"(I) Thence (went) to the Island Ford on the Catawba (River), under a Colonel Farmer where he was in a slight skirmish with the British, and retreated to Torrence's Tavern where they were attacked by the British Cavalry, and retreated from thence to the Adkin (sic Yadkin) River below Salisbury where he joined Main Army under General Greene."

Manuel McConnell 18th September, 1832

" Here we met with Genl. Davidson with some North Carolina Militia & volunteers who applicant thinks has been ordered out for the purpose of preventing the British from crossing the Catawba... (Continued) When Gen. Pickens found Thomas Walters had left his camp on the right bank, he decamped & took the main road leading to Mrs. Torrence, which bored down the

River. But just before (or about the time he) got to Torrence's Cross Roads (Davidson was killed.) Just before an effective step could be taken the British troops rushed on them on the rear and put us completely to rout. After the British had left Mrs. Torrence we rallied our forces there, still under the command of Genl. Pickens & Col. McCall & being pretty much owned Cornwallis's flank until we joined General Greene near Hillsboro."

James Neil 17th December, 1832

" ___ The British forced their way across the Catawba (River) and General Davidson was killed in the action and (the) American Detachment was disbursed___ it was a wet day and on their retreat in small parties they were attacked by the British horse and driven into the swamps __ he (Neil) with some others at last reached Torrens (Torrence's) Tavern where they met Colonel Farmer with upwards of 300 militia"[23]

---

[23] Note: Polly Brandon, Benjamin Carroll, Manuel McConnell, and James Neil's accounts from the database: Pension Application Transcribed by Will Graves- http://revwarapps.org/s31402.pdf (Retrieved: 07/21-24th /2014) Tarleton claim some 500 militia were defending the tavern!

Abraham Forney 31st October, 1832

"Having stood guard at this point and being relieved he went some short distance to a house to obtain refreshments of which he was much in need and was not present when the guard was repulsed and General Davidson killed – with the other troops he fled to the widow Torrence's, where a considerable number of militia had collected – these being defeated and dispersed, that he then fled and joined General Green's [sic, Nathanael Greene's] Army in Guilford County – that from thence he was advised to return home and did so, receiving a ticket to obtain provisions on his return." [24]

One can see that answering 'who was in command' is a difficult challenge. Yet of all the names mentioned throughout the many records, a specific leader at the tavern does come into focus: Colonel Thomas Famer. It is true General Andrew Pickens was is the area and had been at the tavern, but one gets the

---

[24] Ibid. Abraham Forney, W3976 fn 81NC.

impression from several accounts that his troops had already moved away and were acting as the rear guard for General Greene. This force was already between seven to ten miles up the road heading east towards Salisbury around the time of the tavern fight. [25] It was reported that Tarleton's lead units on chasing down tavern defenders did skirmish with a detachment of Pickens' militia before retiring back towards the main body of British troops.[26]

However, it must be mentioned that just because someone is a higher rank does not mean they are automatically in charge when dealing with independent militia bodies at this time. Certainly, military courtesy would be enforced and respected by all groups. Yet, if a lower ranked officer had been given direct command over a specific assignment by the commanding officer (in this case Davidson was the ranking field officer in the entire area), then the lower ranked officer reported and differed to him

[25] If the British had only known how close they were to Greene's Army, American history could have turned out quite different. On can see that Davidson's sacrifice was not in vain!

[26] William R. Reynolds Jr., *Andrew Pickens: South Carolina Patriot in the Revolutionary War*, McFarland and Company Inc., (Jefferson, North Carolina and London 2012) pp. 240-242.

directly. Gen. Davidson being killed that morning does pose a "chain of command" dilemma in this scenario. From several accounts, it seems that the retreating forward troops had just passed the word of Davidson's death when Tarleton's Legion appeared.

My 'professional' view on this issue is that the returning ford troops, and the troops stationed at the tavern, acted under their individual platoon officers and took defensive positions as soon as Tarleton appeared down the road. The Patriot militia realized their duty was to not only slow the British, but to defend refugees who were certainly traveling down the road in the wake of the oncoming British Army. Certainly if Col. Farmer was there with a great number of his militia, he would have held overall command. Farmer probably worked with Gen. Davidson to establish the defensive plans to begin with. Yet I dare say, rank and egos would not have been an issue when a large mounted force of the enemy showed up 'on the doorstep', as it were.

With Tarleton's charge of some estimated 150 to 200 Dragoons, the defenders probably felt the ground shake.[27] The sights and sounds of steel sabres, brass accouterments, and horses would have had a psychological effect on the Patriot militia. For centuries, the cavalry had been the 'shock troops' to pierce any enemy formation. Now at an increasing speed, these 'Green Dragoons' were bearing down on men who probably had time for one or two shots at the most with a flintlock musket before this entire mass came crashing into their lines.

Yet, from Col. Tarleton's report, and from the pension record of Elijah Dollar who mentions that "…. the British Dragoons charged the Americans at Torrence's Tavern several times—and at the time of the second charge, the declarant (Dollar) was taken prisoner by the war." The attack, though swift, was not an easy affair. Even with damp powder, the Patriot militia must have timed their first volley well. It is doubtful that Tarleton would have turned around to rally, but rather would have

---

[27] Note in my work, *The Battle of Cowan's Ford*, the spy report to Davidson estimating around 200 with Tarleton. P. 46. Also: The Davidson College Archives via the British Archive captured papers collection.

'wheeled' left or right not to lose the momentum, and then redirect the attack towards the enemy center. [28]

Tarleton's men pierced the Patriot line, which broke into individual and small parties trying to dodge being sabred or shot. Many broke past the buildings into the woods bordering the main road. Veteran John Lawrence states," ... the British perused & dispersed them completely, some returned home, others were collected in a small body below (the) Yadkin River."[29]

It has been hard over the years to address the casualties of both sides in this battle. Tarleton, no doubt, wanted to boost his image in the official report claiming that some 50 of the Patriot militia were killed outright. Patriot veteran of the battle Arthur Scott claimed that around 30 were either killed or injured.[30] It would probably be safe to say over 20 plus were killed during the engagement, and possibly more died in the following weeks

---

[28] A large group of horses at full speed would have no way of stopping without causing a total disaster, thus mounted troops were trained to shift and divert like a flock of birds.

[29] John Lawrence, Pension Application S31805 state of Georgia, Putnam County, Transcribed by Will Graves- http://revwarapps.org/s31402.pdf (Retrieved: 07/24th /2014)

[30] Arthur Scott, Pension application Ibid. Not-David Henry (Margaret Henry widow pension application 1840), Ibid.

from their injuries. The widow of militiaman David Henry recalled her husband saying that the skirmish was a "great loss of men."

British casualties in the engagement, as reported by Tarleton, were 20 horses and seven men killed. [31] If one factors all of the variable reports, 150-200 Dragoons, and possibly the lead elements of the 23rd Royal Regiment of Foot, attacked some 200-500 Patriot militiamen. I believe it would be safe to conservatively say there were some 500 to 700 total combatants in the skirmish at Torrence's Tavern. In all, a collective number of 30-50 were killed or seriously injured during the action between both belligerents. Tarleton's pursuing troopers probably captured between 10 to 15 Patriots after the action at the tavern had ended. It is clear to see that this "skirmish" was actually a larger battle than many Carolinians had previously believed.

---

[31] Tarleton, p. 226. Note: Tarleton needed supplies (See letter to Gen. Clinton in need of various supplies May 20th, 1781) and would have been less likely to alter his own losses in the hopes of "quartermaster help!"

Aftermath, and the Historic Importance of the Skirmish

It is sometimes hard to put into perspective the importance an event has in the overall scope of history. In my other work, *The Battle of Colson's Mill*, I stress that many of these small skirmishes tallied up in time, and directly impacted the war as much as any large set-piece battle. I think the same thing could be said in the case for the skirmish at Torrence's Tavern. The continued whittling down of British troops, and their support systems, eventually convinced Lord Cornwallis to alter his plans in the American South. After reviewing the many accounts, it is apparent that this 'skirmish' was larger than many previously believed.

Though some men returned to their homes, the pension applications point out many of the tavern defenders headed towards the Yadkin River to join other Patriot forces under General Nathanael Greene and continue the fight. Veteran Elisha Evans actually mentions overtaking Gen. Greene on his way towards Salisbury.[32] Others mention after the skirmish at

Torrence's, they would act as a guerilla force to constantly harass the British in their advance northward. Patriot David Hair recalled they did not despair but continued the fight, "... (Hair) was at the Catawba at the time the British Army in pursuit of Morgan crossed that River, and retreated with the Army to Torrence's (Tavern), where being scattered, and having collected together at Second Creek, fell into the Rear of the British Army and pursued them, and near (the) Dan River joined the Corps under (Gen. Greene)." [33]

For other veterans, the British advance through the region threatened both family and personal property. Patriot John Baldridge's widow Isabella recounted in 1843 her husband's concern for her safety. It is a rare account of the British Army's actions while on the march. Isabella Baldridge's personal commentary on the general scene after Cowan's Ford and Torrence's Tavern is also very touching:

---

[32] Elisha Evans, Pension Application Transcribed by Will Graves-
http://revwarapps.org/s31402.pdf (Retrieved: 07/21/2014) S6830   fn29NC
[33] Ibid, David Hair S6978 fn18NC

" (The) Affiant's husband came to where she was after the retreat (from the tavern) and procured horses and carried her off into a more remote & less dangerous portion of North Carolina." The account goes on to say that, " he (John) was so closely pursued by Cornwallis that she once in the flight had a full view of the British Army. That the British took over their wagon, horses and all their plunder, they afterwards recovered the wagon, but nothing else; and she saw too the unfortunate Davidson after he was killed & her husband called one of her sons William Davidson Baldridge after him. He often spoke of (Davidson) being in numerous scrimmages (and) battles with small parties of Tories and other important services he (Davidson) rendered his Country in the War that gave his country permanent independence." [34]

Mrs. Baldridge also recounts her husband being commissioned as a captain and went on to serve a total of five years during the

[34] John Baldridge, Pension Application Transcribed by Will Graves- http://revwarapps.org/s31402.pdf (Retrieved: 07/21/2014) W5789 fn48NC

war. He was highly respected by other Whigs, and was a pious man. John Baldridge would go on to serve his county after the end of hostilities as a proud American citizen.

When one reads the differing accounts, it becomes clear many of these men served multiple tours of duty during the conflict. It is also important to see their services did not end with the conclusion of the war. Most who survived it would become business leaders in their communities, elders in the local churches, and serve in state government.

Other veterans would be daring, and help pave the way along the frontier in the great westward migration of the early 1800's. I believe this shows the tenacity of the men who fervently believed in their cause. These men had what some might call "true grit." The character traits the veterans of the Revolutionary War displayed became the classic model for many of the American values we hold dear today. Even in this ever-changing world of the 21st Century, many can still admire their traits of community, tenacity, ingenuity, and above all... patriotism.

The Hunt for the Tavern's Location

The area around the Catawba River, and its manmade Lake Norman, has been greatly developed over the past fifty years. This once quiet rural area of North Carolina is now home to a variety of international businesses, relocated employees, their families, and seasonal vacationers. Naturally, this continued development has altered the landscape where much of the fighting occurred. Just past Cowan's Ford, there exists a large hydroelectric dam and power plant. The area where Lord Cornwallis crossed can still be seen while driving across a large bridge that now spans the opposing banks of the river. Yet due to modern security protocols, the public cannot access the area where Gen. Davidson's men made their brave stand. [35]

The exact site Torrence's Tavern has been lost due to development as well. The road that tradition holds Tarelton's

---

[35] Cowan's Ford Island still remains and it is marked on maps reaching back to the time of the battle.

troops pursued the Patriot militia still remains. Langtree Road still closely follows the path as noted on one of the earliest maps that shows the tavern's location. [36] However, it is known that the old "stage road" was altered, possibly due to the development of the modern township of Mount Mourne just a few miles northeast of the tavern's location. Even the original Centre Presbyterian Church where the local militia formed was destroyed. A second building was built and later torn down. The newest worship building (built in 1854) was relocated to the other side of the property. It is a daunting task to say with any certainty where Torrence's Tavern once stood. Yet, there still remain hints as to where it might have been.

A series of articles published in *The Landmark*, between 1911 and 1912 tells the recollections of a Mr. J.W.A. Kerr, Esquire. A Davidson College student (Class of 1855), and a Davidson relative, Mr. Kerr became a local historian of sorts. Mr. Kerr's descriptions are detailed and compelling as to where the tavern was located:

---

[36] Note the 1808 map in the back of this work.

"'Torrence's Tavern' stood about 200 yards northeast of the A.D. Kerr residence, now Dr. Mott's. My father, at the time of my birth, lived on the very spot where Torrence's Tavern stood." Kerr goes on to say that, " The Kerrs of Revolutionary times lived about eight miles northwest of Torrence Tavern, near the present station of Mount Mourn on the Atlantic, Tennessee and Ohio (Statesville and Charlotte) railroad. " He even states that, " The Templetons lived on the east side of Davidson Creek, about 1 ½ mile from Torrence's Tavern, and some of their lands are still in the family." [37]

Mr. Kerr's article further tells of the founding families of the region. Houston, Templetons, Kerrs, Davidsons, and the Whites are few mentioned in his recollections.[38] Given his age, I am sure that as a young boy he might have heard from people in the range of his grandparent's generation that would have

---

[37] J.W. A. Kerr, *The Landmark*, September 26, 1911. (The Genealogical Society of Iredell County, NC Collection)

[38] The same family that produced Gen. Sam Houston of Texas.

remembered where the tavern once stood. One gets the impression of a true local authority while reading his commentaries. Even with such details, the entire area of the tavern has been landscaped and developed, mostly in the last half of the 20th Century. Mr. Kerr would scarcely recognize the area if he was alive today.

One thing Mr. Kerr does not address directly is which of the many Torrences actually owned the tavern? For years it was debated. Yet with good research methodology, I believe I can say with a great degree of certainty which Torrence was the tavern owner/keep. General Graham's account published in 1904 specifically stated that "... widow Torrence; her husband had been killed at the battle of Ramsour's Mill...."[39] While researching the pension files I realized there were as many uses of the word Tarrants and Terrence as there was Torrence. I also knew there were two Torrences listed at Centre Presbyterian Church as members of the colonial militia; an Adam Torrence Sr. and Adam Torrence Jr. I then searched for Adam 'Tarrants' and

---

[39] Graham, p.300.

"Terrence" using the other spellings to see what might show up. What I found was a pension application dated October 5th, 1824 under the name of Adam Terrence. It is an application of a crippled but proud man who did not want to ask for any assistance. One can tell that the memories he recounts for the court are painful. In his follow up supportive letter to the court a month later, he tells of the sudden death of his father in battle, and the pains he has lived with all of his life due to the injury he received in the same brutal engagement:

" Mount Mourn No. Ca. 30th Novr. 1824

Dear Sir

Enclosed you will find my papers relative to my application for a pension- I am now old & worn out, a small matter of gratitude from my Country for a very little space of time would help me much being much disabled from the effects of a wound received during the revolutionary War at the Battle Ramsour's (Mill) Lincoln County (Lincolnton) where I saw my Father fall on the field of Battle being shot dead through the head by a ball & a few moments afterwards I was shot in the hip & which hurt me all of my life since, but so long as I help power to labor I declined asking- now forced by entire disability to labor in my shop or else where (being bred a Blacksmith) & having a large family of females (six all grown) & but one small son now living with me you must see that my situation would thankfully receive that assistance that is due to a Soldier & in the cause of Liberty & national independence lost that means which would still enabled me in some (way?) to have worked for the support of my family heretofore-..." [40]

- Adam Terrence (jr.)

Having found this story in the pension application, along with a confirmation that an Adam Tarrance (Sr.) had applied for a tavern license prior to the Revolutionary War as recorded in the

---

[40] Adam Terrence, Pension Application Transcribed by Will Graves-
http://revwarapps.org/s31402.pdf (Retrieved: 07/25/2014) S14663 fn32NC. Note: After the war a second tavern was built and referred to as "Cross Keys" yet in time it was dismantled. I found no reference to the original tavern as "Cross Keys" during my research. "The Statesville Daily," Sept. 23, 1940; and "The State," March 29, 1941. Also note William S. Powell's description of the rebuilt tavern in the *Mooresville Tribune* Nov. 6, 1947. He notes that "Cross Keys" was a two-story dwelling, with six Doric columns, with a lean-to, and a kitchen out back. Presumably, the chimney was original to the tavern burned by the British. Yet, Powell refers back to Wheeler's account of the engagement.

Rowan County records, solidified my opinion that we had finally found the man, even if we had yet to find his tavern.[41]

There are still people today on a quest to pinpoint the tavern's location. I too have been pulled into the search. During my research on the Battle of Colson's Mill, I was amazed that a roadbed could still exist from the Revolutionary Era.[42] What really attracted my attention was the fact that satellite imagining revealed topographical details no one could possibly see from the ground. After a friend forwarded an 1808 map showing the roads, Centre Presbyterian Church, and the Tavern's location, I decided to put modern technology to work.

Factoring all I knew of the changes and existing landmarks, I did run across something strange. A noticeable path way that followed parallel to Langtree Road right past The Cove Church. After backing out of Google Earth around 1000 feet, I noticed this path could be seen stretching in the general direction of Salisbury and beyond. Upon further research, it turned out that

---

[41] See: Jo White Linn, *Abstracts of the Minutes of the Court of Pleas and Quarter Sessions Rowan County, North Carolina, 1763-1774* (n.p. 1979), pp. 89, 119, 146, and 160. Also listing later in this work.

[42] The King's Road on the Colson property, Norwood NC.

was the Transco Pipeline installed several decades ago. This line is one of the greatest suppliers of natural gas along the east coast. It was a dead end... or so I thought. A few days later, I started thinking a bit deeper when I realized this line was installed during the time of the creation of Lake Norman. That would mean survey teams would have to have been sent out, maps made, strata surveys, and possibly photographic work. Whole forested areas would have to be cleared for the pipe's installation. That takes time and money. What if a survey team noticed a cleared path (or old roadbed) already close to the route where the line was to be installed?

It made sense to me if a road went for miles within the planned route of the pipeline, certainly for cost alone, would it not be used? I decided to contact Transco directly and tactfully ask if they would possibly have aerial pictures, records, or old survey maps prior to instillation. I also realized that, possibly due to security reasons, I might receive a standard automated reply and denial. What I did receive back was rather enlightening. Keeping in mind that sometimes it is what is not

stated in a letter that tells more:

January 26th 2014 (e-mail)

Begin forwarded message: the pipeline and old trails?

Mr. Stonestreet,

I was forwarded your email to contact our local personnel and checked in the division office to see if we could provide any assistance in your request. It sounds like an intriguing challenge. After contacting our local personnel and reviewing what we have in the division office, I sorry to say we do not have any information/photography, etc. that may provide assistance.

I do wish you luck in your endeavor.

Jim Hutchins
Sr. Land Representative

The grand stone marker that the Mary Slocumb Chapter of the

DAR placed at the end of Langtree Road in 1914 is certainly close

to where the tavern once stood; and certainly less than half a

mile at most. In 2014, this stone marker was refurbished and

rededicated by the DAR to the brave men who made their stand that fateful afternoon on February 1st, 1781. Yet, finding the 'exact spot' where the tavern stood now would be a stroke of luck. Lowe's Corporate Headquarters owns property that might hold some clues, yet they understandably do not want people traipsing across their property. Other companies see the risks of a weekend historian possibly getting injured on their property, and having to cover medical cost should an accident happen. Who knows what may still turn up as time goes on? For it seems history likes to uncover a surprise once and a while. As for myself, and others, the hunt still goes on.

NC State Marker - M5 Torrence's Tavern

Patriot Ladies: Then and Now

An unsung group who certainly played their part in the skirmish Torrence's Tavern were the women of the community. Unlike battles of today that usually take place hundreds or even thousands of miles away, these women were seeing the men of their families face the possibility of death right down the road. They knew the men were fighting to protect those they held dearest, and yet it still did not lessen the pain of uncertainty as the enemy approached.

Women's roles in the American Revolution ranged greatly. Often mothers, wives, and daughters volunteered to tend to the injured. Many ladies cooked, cleaned, made ammunition, spied and even fought at times. The women of the community around Torrence's Tavern, like thousands of other ladies across the nation, certainly supported the Patriot cause. One only has to remember the tavern was still fully operating and referred to as "Widow Torrence's Tavern" well over a month after the death of her husband at Ramsour's Mill. With a garrison of 300 or more militia as a secondary defensive line stationed at the tavern, there is no question the ladies played an important role in supporting them. As mentioned earlier, the tavern served as a storehouse as well as a center for the gathering Patriots in the days leading up to the battle on the Catawba. During every American conflict going back to the Revolutionary War, women bore a great deal of responsibility tending to the home, businesses and family as the men were away. As in all wars, due to the labor shortage, women often stepped out of their traditional roles to do jobs that were normally held by men.

Many people believe the number of people filling the roads ahead of the British advance were purely refugees; families fleeing in fear. However, when one reads the various accounts, and realizes the scale of the battle, it becomes clear a percentage of women fleeing west after the British attack were actively involved with supporting the Patriot camp and the tavern itself.

As in the past, many ladies across the nation are still actively involved with the Patriot cause. Since 1890, the National Society Daughters of the American Revolution, or DAR, have dedicated themselves to persevering our nation's history. Likewise, not far from the battlefield of Torrence's Tavern, the Mary Slocumb Chapter of DAR formed in Mooresville, North Carolina on October 1st 1903.[43] For over a hundred years, this chapter has brought public attention to the efforts and sacrifices that were made by those in the American Revolution. In 1914, the Mary Slocumb Chapter dedicated a large stone monument to the memory of those that fought at Torrence's Tavern. One must remember it took donated funds to have the marker carved, moved and erected. It would be many years before a state funded historical marker would be placed near the DAR marker just off of Langtree Road.

In 2014, the Torrence's Tavern DAR marker was removed, refurbished, and reinstalled. A new base was added, and the marker has been placed in a more prominent location near the old site. It still stands as a testament to those who served at this important engagement of the Revolutionary War. I was fortunate to be present when the newly cleaned marker was

___

[43] http://www.ncdar.org/MarySlocumb_files/html/history.html (Retrieved: 09/09/2014)

reinstalled. Besides a small number of men, mostly police and the reinstallation crew, I realized that few men were there of their own accord. Yet, many members of the Mary Slocumb Chapter were in attendance on this very warm summer day. It then dawned on me, though the Patriot militias are long gone, it is the ladies who are still holding the line at Torrence's Tavern.

DAR Torrence's Tavern Marker Rededication
20th, September 2014
MSHS NJROTC Color Guard

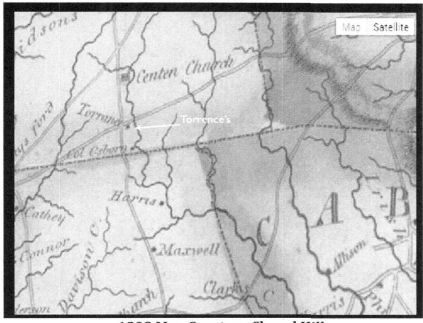

**1808 Map Courtesy Chapel Hill
Wilson Special Collections Library**

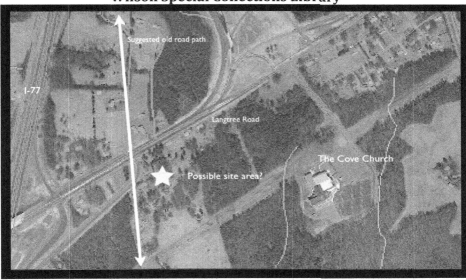

2010 Survey Map- Courtesy of Iredell County GIS

Centre Presbyterian Church (1854 Building)
Mooresville, NC

The Rededicated 1914 DAR Marker

Known Tarrant's/Torrence's Tavern Patriot Defenders
(Incomplete list)

Name	Rank	
Alexander Aston	Lt.	
James Aston		
John Baldridge	Capt.	
John Baldwin		
Benjamin Brandon		
Robert Brevard		Probable
William Brown		
Benjamin Carroll		
Jonas Clark		
John Cobb		
Thomas Cowan	Capt.	
Elijah Dollar		Captured
Elisha Evans		
Abraham Forney		
James Gresham		
David Hair		
Solomon Hall		
David Henry	Lt.	
James Holmes		
Issac Holeman		
Thomas Hustchins		
John Laurence		
Thomas Lesly		
Elias Lovelace		
Salatheil/Nathaniel Martin	**Capt.**	
* Mentioned by Graham (Captured)		
Manuel McConnell		
Robert McCormick		

Charles McIntosh
James Mitchell
James Neil
Patrick Norris
Joseph Newton
Joseph Patten
John Patterson
Andrew Pickens   South Carolina Col. /Gen.
John Porterfield
Benjamin Shaw
Peter Skeen
Arthur Scott
Richard Smith
Joshua Spears
Jonathan Starky
John Stonecypher
John Swanson
James Wilson

Persons of Special Note-

1. Capt. Salathiel/Nathaniel Martin (captured) was reportedly 6 feet 9 inches tall. His widow Mary Cook (remarried) did not file for a pension until she was 93 years old in 1857. There was no mention in her deposition of the tavern, but a general account of his actions under Gen. Greene. Note: Some accounts state that Capt. Martin's brother might have been with him as a Lt. under his brother's command at the tavern. [44]

2. Col. Thomas Famer- Several sources claim that farmer was at the tavern during the action leading his militia. * See Farmer's letter to Gen. Greene included in this work.

---

[44] Salathiel/Nathaniel Martin (Widow Mary's Deposition) Pension Application Transcribed by Will Graves- http://revwarapps.org/s31402.pdf (Retrieved: 07/20/2014) W1044 fn120NC

3. Gen. Andrew Pickens was commanding regional Patriot forces after Gen. Davidson's death. He had only been recently promoted to the rank of general.

4. Adam Terrence (Torrence) Jr. may have been at Cowan's Ford and the tavern skirmish. Yet, it is not recounted in any of the records that I came across.

5. Valentine Tuder- **Pension Excerpt**: *"On the same day of the battle at Catawba, there was an engagement at Mrs. Torrern's (Tavern) with the British. Deponent (I) was not in it, but was guarding some Tory prisoners about a mile and a half off. That he knows of no person, whose testimony he can procure, who can testify to his service except his brother John Tuder. "*

(Mr. Tuder was with Davidson's detachment, but was not at Torrence's during the battle due to being on guard duty! It is the only instance of Tory interaction during the Cowan's Ford crossing other than the supposed Tory guide for Lord Cornwallis).[45]

---

[45] Ibid. Valentine Tuder, (Retrieved 08/07/2014) S30755 fn34NC Note: spelling- Torrens.

"Col. Thomas Farmer to Gen. Greene- Camp Near Salisbury 22nd, Jan. 1781

Sir,

Our number of Troops from Hillsborough District being noways Compleat, Have Ordered a Capt & Leut to Collect the Guard you appd out of the Delinquents. The Troops under my Command Concist of about 310 Including Officers Soldiers & Wagoners. We have Seven Wagons, Two Thousand four Hundred Cartridges[,] Two Hundred & forty Muskets, One Hundred & Thirty Eight Bayonets, One Hundred & fifteen C[artridge] Boxes[,] forty nine Knap Sacks, Thirty five Pots, Twelve axes and Thirty-six flints. We Expected to be furnished with flints at this post, & all other Articles Sutable for Camp, but Cannot. Have Sent to Gen l Davidson for flints & his Answer is also Doubtfull, Concerning them.
Have recd Ord[e]rs from Gen l Davidson to Joyn him as Quick as possible. Shall March at 12 OClock to day to Joyn him. Am Sir, with Respect
yr Hb l Servt

Thos Farmer (Thomas Farmer)"[46]

---

[46] *The Papers of General Nathanael Greene*, ed. Dennis Conrad et al. (Columbia, S.C.: Model Editions Partnership, 1999). Full texts of documents calendared in *The Papers of General Nathanael Greene* (Chapel Hill, N.C.: University of North Carolina Press, 1994), Vol. 7, pp. 152-289. On the Web at http://mep.blackmesatech.com/mep/ [Accessed 13 May 2014] and Retrieved : 08/17/2014 via
http://wyatt.elasticbeanstalk.com/mep/NG/xml/ng07169c.html

Centre Presbyterian Church Patriot Militia

James Houston, Capt.
William Davidson, Lieut.
David Eavins (*sic* Evans?) Lieut.
David Byers
Robert Byers
Nathaniel Ewing
Alexander Work
William Creswell
William Erwin
John Caldwell
Joseph Mc Cawn (*sic* Mc Cowan)
James Young
James Gray
Philip Logan
William Kint
Daniel Bryson
John Singleton
John Beard
John Cunningham
Paul Cunningham
Moses White
John Hovis
John Poston
Robert Poston
Charles Quigley
Adam Torrence, Sr.   (Tavern owner-Killed at the Battle of
Ramsour's Mill)
Adam Torrence, Jr.   Lieut. (later promoted)
Thomas Templeton
John McConnells
Angus McAuley
John Thompson
Benjamin Brevard
Robert Brevard

James Gulic

IN MEMORY OF REVOLUTIONARY SOLDIERS
WHO ENLISTED FROM CENTRE CONGREGATION
1775 —— 1781.

JAMES HOUSTON,Capt. WILLIAM DAVIDSON,Lieut. DAVID EAVINS,Lieut.
DAVID BYERS.   ROBERT POSTON.   BENJAMIN BREVARD.
ROBERT BYERS.   PAUL CUNNINGHAM.   THOMAS TEMPLETON.
NATHANIEL EWING.   JOHN CUNNINGHAM.   JOHN CALDWELL.
ALEXANDER WORK.   JOHN McCONNELS.   JOSEPH McCAWN.
WILLIAM CRESWELL.   MOSES WHITE.   JAMES YOUNG.
WILLIAM ERWIN.   ANGUS McAULEY.   PHILIP LOGAN.
JOHN HOVIS.   ROBERT BREVARD.   WILLIAM KINT.
JOHN THOMPSON.   ADAM TORRENCE,Sr.   DANIEL BRYSON.
JOHN BEARD.   ADAM TORRENCE,Jr.   JOHN SINGLETON.
JOHN POSTON.   CHARLES QUIGLY.   JAMES GRAY.
                      JAMES GULIC.
PLACED BY MARY SLOCUMB CHAPTER
DAUGHTERS OF THE AMERICAN REVOLUTION.
1914.

**Centre Presbyterian Church Militia Honor Plaque- Near
Torrence's Tavern
(Original ranks at the time of organization)
Photo Courtesy: Rhonda Sherrill**

Adam Torrence Sr. (Tarrance, Tarance etc.)
Tavern License

The following information is from: White, Jo Linn, *Abstracts of the Minutes of the Court of Pleas and Quarter Sessions Rowan County, North Carolina, 1763-1774* (1979):

P.89   Deed from Adam Torrence to Hugh Torrence for 311 acres. 13 Nov. 1768 (7:381) Order that Adam Torrence to have Lycens to keep a tavern at his own dwelling in Rowan County. Alexr Osborn and CHS Purvians sec. in Sum L30.

P.119 3: 245 Adam Tarrance renews tavern license with Capt. John Oliphant and Chas Purviance securities John Lewis Beard does also with Geo Hen Barager as security. (1771)

P.146. 4 Feb. 1773 Adam Tarance Licensed to keep tavern at his house, Francis Lock, John Oliphant securities.

* **Note on spelling**: As noted in the other parts of this work, there are various spellings and pronunciations of the name Torrence. Mainly due to the inconsistent levels of education of those recording the information. Also, there may have been various pronunciations given different regional dialects. This may account for some of the spelling issues.

Standardized Tavern Rates in the 1770s (Rowan/Rohan County) NC

Product/Service	Pounds, Shillings, Pence
Gallon of West Indian Rum	0.16.0
New England Rum	0.10.8
Brandy and Whiskey	0.10.0
Beer (with 4 busheld Malt & Hops to barrel), p. Qt.	0.00.6
Peach Brandy or Whiskey mad into cordial , p gill	0.00.4
Sheaf oats, p sheaf of 5 in, diameter	0.00.4
Sheaf fodded by sheaf of well-cured bound U in. diameter	0.00.4
Beer with 5 bu. 3 mo. Old per qt.	0.00.8
Qt. of Toddy made of west Indian rum with loaf sugar	0.01.4
Pt of sling made the same	0.01.4
Pt of sling made of New England rum	0.01.0
Ditto of Brandy or whiskey	0.01.0
Madeira or Vidonia wine per gallon	0.16.0
Sanger with loaf sugar per quart	0.01.4
Horse stabling 24 hrs. with plenty of hay or fodder In common woodshed.	0.00.8
If English grass such as Timothy or Clover Corn or Oats p. qt.	0.00.2
Breakfast or supper with hot meat & small drink	0.00.8
Ditto with coffee	0.01.0
Dinner with a Sufficient Dish of Wholesome well Dressed and well served up meat.	0.01.0
Good pasture for a horse for night.	0.00.8
Lodging P(er) night good bed & clean sheets	0.00.4
Boiled Cyder P Quart	0.00.8
Cyder Royal P Quart	0.01.4
Draught Cyder P Quart	0.00.8
Clarrett P Bottle	0.07.6
Punch P Qt. with Orange or Lime juice	0.02.0

Likewise for larger or smaller quantities. Rates to remain the same until altered.
(Circa 1774)

"Sling" is a drink that was made of a shot of brandy, whiskey, gin or rum combined with lemon juice, sugar/honey or syrup plus an ale. Sling is like a toddy with spices. The term sling comes from the German word "Schlingen" or "to swallow" [47]

Source: White, Jo Linn, *Abstracts of the Minutes of the Court of Pleas and Quarter Sessions Rowan County, North Carolina, 1763-1774* (1979). P. 161.

---

[47] Difford's Guide, http://www.diffordsguide.com/cocktails/recipe/1830/sling-generic-name (Retrieved: 08/16/2014)

Sources

Bass, Robert D.,*The Green Dragoon: The Lives of Banastre Tarleton and Mary Robinson*, (Orangeburg: Sandlapper Publishing Co. Inc., 1973)

Conrad, Dennis ed. *The Papers of General Nathanael Greene*, et al. (Columbia, S.C.: Model Editions Partnership, 1999). Full texts of documents calendared in *The Papers of General Nathanael Greene* (Chapel Hill, N.C.: University of North Carolina Press, 1994), Vol. 7, pp. 152-289.

Charles Cornwallis, *Correspondence of Charles, First Marquis Cornwallis*, Charles Derek Ross (editor) Volume 1. (Cambridge: Cambridge University Press- first edition 1859) Reprint 2011.

_____ Letter to George Sackville Germain, Viscount Sackville, Cornwallis, Charles Cornwallis, Marquis, 1738-1805 March 17, 1781 Volume 17, Pages 995-1001 Colonial and State Records of North Carolina.
http://docsouth.unc.edu/csr/index.html/document/csr17-0307 (Retrieved: 08/04/2014).

Graham, William A., *General Joseph Graham and his Papers on North Carolina Revolutionary History; with Appendix: An Epitome of North Carolina's Military Services in the Revolutionary War and of the Laws Enacted for Raising Troops,* Miami: HardPress Publishing, (Print on Demand 2013), 1904 ed.

Graves, Will, Pension Applications-Transcriptionist, Database: http://revwarapps.org/s31402.pdf (Pension Retrievals: 07/19/2014- 08/23/2014)

Kerr, W.A., *Old Centre Church Congregation*, The Landmark, Tuesday, Sept. 26th, 1911.

_____ . *The Landmark*, April 15th, 1912.

Reynolds, William R. Jr., *Andrew Pickens: South Carolina Patriot in the Revolutionary War*, McFarland and Company Inc., (Jefferson, North Carolina and London 2012)

Stonestreet, O.C. IV, *The Battle of Cowan's Ford: General Davidson's Stand on the Catawba River and its Place in North Carolina History*, (Createspace, Charleston, 2012).

Tarleton, Lieutenant-General CN, *A History of the Campaigns of 1780 and 1781, in the Southern Provinces of North America*, London, 1787, (Reprint- Public Domain, 2014).

Thorp, Daniel B., Taverns and Tavern Culture on the Southern Colonial Frontier: Rowan County, North Carolina, 1753-1776. *The Journal of Southern History,* Vol. 62. No. 4 (Nov., 1996), PP. 661-688. http://www.jstor.org/stable/2211137. Retrieved: 19/12/ 2013.

White, Jo Linn, *Abstracts of the Minutes of the Court of Pleas and Quarter Sessions Rowan County, North Carolina, 1763-1774* (n.p. 1979).

Made in the USA
Middletown, DE
24 December 2022

17410386R00046